YOUR SPECIAL GRANDCHILD

Your Special Grandchild

**A Book for Grandparents of Children
Diagnosed with Asperger Syndrome**

JOSIE SANTOMAURO

Illustrated by Carla Marino

Jessica Kingsley Publishers
London and Philadelphia

First published in 2009
by Jessica Kingsley Publishers
116 Pentonville Road
London N1 9JB, UK
and
400 Market Street, Suite 400
Philadelphia, PA 19106, USA

www.jkp.com

Copyright © Josie Santomauro 2009
Illustrations copyright © Carla Marino 2009

Library of Congress Cataloging in Publication Data
Santomauro, J. (Josie)
    Your special grandchild : a book for grandparents of children diagnosed with Asperger
syndrome / Josie Santomauro ; illustrated by Carla Marino.
        p. cm.
    ISBN 978-1-84310-659-3 (pb : alk. paper) 1. Asperger's syndrome--Popular works.
2. Asperger's syndrome--Patients--Family relationships. 3. Parents of autistic children. 4.
Grandparents. I. Marino, Carla. II. Title.
    RJ506.A9S3673 2009
    618.92'858832--dc22
                                                        2008041359

British Library Cataloguing in Publication Data
A CIP catalogue record for this book is available from the British Library

ISBN 978 1 84310 659 3

Printed and bound in Great Britain by
Athenaeum Press, Gateshead, Tyne and Wear

To Nonna and Nonno
Understanding grandparents

I wish to thank all the wonderful
contributors who have given
permission to reprint their gifts of
poetry, reflections, writings and
private thoughts here in this
book.

Contents

Introduction

I congratulate you on reaching this point, to move on from the initial diagnosis of your grandchild having Asperger Syndrome.

Your grandchild may have been given the diagnosis of Asperger Syndrome by a pediatrician or child psychologist. A therapist, teacher or friend may have initiated the diagnosis journey. I hope that you and the child's parents were dealt the news in a compassionate and positive way.

Diagnosis is the first hurdle and there will be many more hurdles in your grandchild's life. The end result is the satisfaction that you were there for your grandchild. Friends, doctors, teachers will come and go, but you will be part of the team that offers the stability in his/her life, and you will have made a difference. Your role as grandparent is not only to help your grandchild understand, accept and love the world, but to help people around your grandchild to understand, accept and love your grandchild's world.

Although Asperger Syndrome may appear to consume the parents' lives sometimes (well, most of the time) try to help them to not dwell on the negatives, but to love the positives and embrace their child's successes.

The aim of this book is to introduce Asperger Syndrome to you in a positive light, and to guide you, the grandparent, through some issues that you may face on the Asperger Syndrome journey with your grandchild.

My son, Damian, was diagnosed 13 years ago, at the age of five, therefore I am able to share my first-hand experiences.

We can learn from those who have already started this journey as I have learned from others also.

I encourage you to research and learn as much about Asperger Syndrome as you can, to equip yourself with the tools to support your grandchild and their parents. There is a list of useful websites on p.46.

Best wishes and good luck!

What is Asperger Syndrome?

There are various ways of defining Asperger Syndrome. Practising clinical psychologist and Asperger Syndrome specialist, Tony Attwood, describes it as 'someone who perceives and thinks about the world differently to other people'. I can only offer you basic information on the diagnostic area, but a wealth of information based on my experiences. I encourage you to seek further information from specialists, support groups, other parents, other grand-parents, the internet and other resources. Knowledge is power – I can't state this enough. The more you learn, the more adept you will become in handling your grandchild's journey.

Throughout this book you will find Asperger Syndrome referred to as AS, and sometimes as an ASD. ASD is an abbreviation for autism spectrum disorder. Asperger Syndrome falls within the autistic spectrum.

On first meeting someone we make a number of judgements. We can tell their age and a lot about their character from their appearance, and we can tell from facial expressions and tone of voice what mood they are in. This enables us to react to them in an appropriate way.

People with AS don't find it so easy to recognize this information, and because they find eye contact difficult it is hard for them to interact easily with other people.

However, once they are diagnosed with AS, these difficulties can be understood and dealt with, and the benefits of AS can be appreciated.

What's wrong with my grandchild?

Your grandchild needs extra assistance in these four areas:

1. Social skills
2. Communication
3. Behaviour
4. Sensory stimulation.

Social skills

Two-way social interaction may be impaired due to the inability of your grandchild to understand the rules of social behaviour. There may be little or no eye contact used when listening or speaking. A lack of empathy may be shown to others and to others' interests/activities, unless they are of specific interest to your grandchild.

Communication

Your grandchild may speak at the appropriate age, but sometimes speech is delayed. Speech may be pedantic and/or repetitive. Usually there are comprehension difficulties with verbal instructions, etc. He/she tends to be a very visual thinker and learner.

Behaviour

Your grandchild may become obsessive about particular possessions or objects. Preferring life to be predictable they don't cope well with change in situations, structure or routine. They do not cope well with verbal instructions, therefore to avoid negative feedback they can become defiant in their behaviour.

Sensory stimulation

Your grandchild may have difficulty focusing attention due to hyper- or hypo-sensory input in the environment (e.g. they may need headphones in noisy places). They may need sensory experiences built into the day (e.g. stress balls or other fidget items).

Common features of Asperger Syndrome

A nger and frustration

S tress and anxiety

P roblems with speech and language

E asily distracted

R eality/Fiction confusion

G ross motor skills

E ccentric or odd behaviours

R igid and resistant to change

S ocial skills deficit

Y our grandchild may be intelligent

N o or little eye contact

D oesn't like loud noises and crowds

R ote memory strong

O bsessional interests

M aking friends may be difficult

E mpathy – lack of

Let's take a closer look at Asperger Syndrome

Anger and frustration

- Your grandchild may have temper tantrums or anger outbursts.

- They might find it hard to ask for help when feeling confused or frustrated.

Stress and anxiety

- They don't cope well with being teased or bullied.

- They are sometimes anxious over changes.

- They are often very stressed at school.

- They don't cope well with criticism or failure.

Problems with speech and language

- They may not realize that their voice is too loud.

- They may have a monotone voice or an unusual accent.

- They may require some speech therapy.

- They may have difficulty explaining what they want to say.

Easily distracted

- Maybe their room and school desk is untidy.

- They may have short-term memory problems.

- It can be hard for them to pay attention or focus.

Reality/Fiction confusion

- Sometimes they don't understand jokes or stories.

- They may believe that their dreams are real.

- They take things literally, such as 'pull your socks up', and don't understand sarcasm.

Gross motor skills

- They may appear clumsy or have an odd gait.
- They may have poor co-ordination and find some sports (especially ball games) challenging.

Eccentric or odd behaviours

- They may have eccentric/odd behaviours.
- They may have eccentric/odd collections/hobbies.

Rigid and resistant to change

- They prefer routine and structure.
- They work best when forewarned about events.
- They may not work well with transitions.

Social skills deficit

- They may find it hard to understand people's body language.
- They need help to ignore teasing and bullying.
- They may be unaware of social rules and can sometimes appear rude.

Your grandchild may be intelligent

- They can be very intelligent – especially at maths, science and computers.

- They are nicknamed 'little professor' by some professionals.

No or little eye contact

- They don't like looking into people's eyes when they talk to them and may look at the ground instead of someone's face.

- They may find the ground more interesting than your face but they are still listening to what you are saying.

Doesn't like loud noises and crowds

- They are sensitive to sensory stimuli.
- Noisy or crowded places, like shopping centres or parties, can overload their sensory system.

Rote memory strong

- Excellent long-term memory.
- Walking encyclopedia for specific facts.

Obsessional interests

- An obsession with a particular hobby/subject can dominate conversations, play and daily life.

- Repetitive movements, e.g. flapping their hands, touching their face or blinking.

Making friends may be difficult

- They might not have many friends and find it hard to make new friends.

- They may not have a desire to have friends, they may prefer to be on their own.

- They may prefer to play with older or younger people.

Empathy – lack of

- Sometimes they can't understand how other people are feeling.

- They may find it difficult to understand facial expressions.

Here's another acrostic to show some other characteristics of Asperger Syndrome:

A rtistic

S mart

P unctual

E ngaging

R epetitive movements

G ood natured

E xtraordinary

R ules

S ignificant

Y why? Asks lots of questions

N atural

D etermined

R esourceful

O ver sensitive

M aths wiz

E motional

Good Grief

When a parent is told their child has a disability they need to go through the classic stages of grief. If they put the process on hold they may find that a breakdown may eventually hit years later, particularly for mothers.

Grief is the natural healing process of a loss. You as a grandparent may also grieve the news of your grandchild's diagnosis. You may also be crucial to helping the parent in their grieving period. Allow them to grieve. It's healthy to grieve. It's a health hazard to bury your emotions.

Grief comes with a sense of loss, either of a loved one, a job, pet, home or physical action. Even aging can cause grief. So the grief experienced at the loss of the 'normality' of a child can have the same impact as these other losses. A diagnosis of a disability, disease or life-threatening illness can have a devastating effect on the whole family.

The diagnosis of a child with Asperger Syndrome can have the same impact on a family as news of a death.

The grieving process begins, and it is important that the family is allowed to grieve in their own way. Each person should take the necessary time to grieve, without pressure to 'pick themselves up'. It is very important that support is in place to assist the grieving process along.

These are some feelings/behaviours you may be experiencing:

- denial
- shock
- anger
- guilt
- regret
- depression
- loneliness.

There are many changes about to happen to the family of a newly diagnosed child. They will gradually learn to understand and accommodate these changes and move on to a different path.

The stages of grief are denial, anger, sadness and then, finally, acceptance.

Denial: The initial shock. It's difficult to believe what you've just been told. 'This can't be happening to us.'

Anger: The most difficult stage. 'It's not fair, why us?' This stage introduces feelings of guilt, 'What have we done to deserve this?' Self-blame may become a problem, or you may blame doctors, schools, etc. Anger may also be directed at the child.

Sadness: The essential ingredient of the grieving process. Cry, cry and more crying, it's good for the process, don't hold back, don't swallow it.

Acceptance: Resuming life. Getting back to the way things were prior to diagnosis but on a different level. This is the sign that the grieving process is nearing the end.

It may take more than six months to grieve or it may take some years, but the process is essential. Blocking it or not allowing grief will only create problems later, e.g. breakdown/depression.

Friends and family may try to make the family feel better by saying things like: 'It's not the end of the world'/'Life goes on'/'Be strong'. These aren't exactly the things the family wants to hear at the time, but they mean well. Finding a friend or support group who will help the family and listen is very beneficial.

Why has my grandchild got Asperger Syndrome?
The best specialists still don't really know the exact answer to this question. Research and studies are ongoing.

It may be genetic, it may be due to the mother contracting a virus whilst pregnant, or it may be that the child contracts a virus in their first year.

With my son, it could have been any or all three of the above:

1. I think there may be some family members with mild traits.

2. At 22 weeks pregnant, I contracted a virus and was hospitalized due to dehydration.

3. At 11 months, Damian contracted the measles virus (one month before he was due for the immunization). He was very sick, and it took him about two months to recover. When he did get better, he reverted to crawling.

Asperger Syndrome is not caught like a cold, that glass of wine does not cause it during pregnancy, and it's not because your grandchild fell and hit their head. Some say it's possibly due to immunizations, some say there's a possible dietary factor. Until the day the discovery of the cause is officially announced, I believe we should just move on and deal with the symptoms.

What we do know is that there is at least one in every 150 people who has Asperger Syndrome and, most importantly, through communication with adults with Asperger Syndrome, we do know how to make their lives easier and we can gain a better understanding of their world.

We now have to teach the world to accept them and their ways.

Been There, Done That

Learning from those who have been there before, those who have paved the way (whether they be other mothers, grandparents or adults with ASD), can be empowering in knowledge as well as reassuring to those just beginning to find their feet.

I have found that the words from adults with ASD are precious, and by listening to them you can be guided with your decision-making when confronted by situations with your own grandchildren.

Please enjoy the contributions and in particular the article written by Rick and Marlene Anthony from the United States. I feel that any grandparent of a child with a disability can relate to these stories about their grandchildren.

Your grandchild

Your grandchild is still the same person they were before the diagnosis. You love them and they love you, even if they cannot show it. They have so many good qualities. Celebrate those good qualities and help them work through difficult areas. You are an anchor and interpreter in the 'normal' world.

Marie Hoder (Nashville, TN, USA) Mother of a child with AS/ADD

Asperger never leaves

Asperger Syndrome if you have it never leaves, in actual fact it never gets better! There is no cure, but as we get older we learn new ways around corners.

Circumstances alter and we may be given advice in coping strategies and that is what it is, just coping. In the end, we devise methods of getting around those corners on our own. Sometimes we do it well, sometimes not, but anybody who lives in close contact knows that we have not really changed, but that we still have those problems.

It is only those people who are not close to us that can be fooled. The key words here being 'close to us', as we tend not to develop closeness with many people.

Rest assured that the day will never dawn when you will awaken to find ASD on any level gone.

Yes, your grandchild will probably need help in mainstream school, and as he gets older will probably need more help, not less.

Nanna Shirl (Gin Gin, Australia) 'An old dyed in the wool –
age early seventies' with Asperger Syndrome

I too, believe that understanding is really the biggest thing that we all wish for.

All my life I can remember yelling at my parents…

'You just don't understand me…'

Then came the tantrums.

Judy Darcy (Melbourne, Australia)
Adult with Asperger Syndrome

My life with Asperger

It is difficult to find the words to describe the effects of Asperger Syndrome, in order for people who are NT (Neurologically typical) to understand. The problem is that not being NT, I don't know what their experience is like. Of course, communication is a major problem for people with Asperger Syndrome.

Over the years, I have learned to cope with AS whilst not knowing I had it. I only found out in early 2000. I have forced myself to look people in the eye when I talk to them, as well as to take part in conversations with people whilst attempting to give the impression that I am empathetic. I can sympathize with people to a certain extent but I don't have direct access to my emotions. I sometimes use the wrong emotional response. I also cannot manage my facial expressions. If someone asks me to smile, for instance, I can't, unless I have access to a mirror. Empathy just doesn't come naturally to me. I also have to keep a watch on my tendency to steer the conversation around to my interests all the time.

I have problems deciding when to start speaking in a conversation, so I tend to interrupt the other person constantly. If several people are having a conversation and attempt to include me, I find it so focusing that I can't keep up with the conversation. By the time I have thought of something to say the topic has usually moved on. My thinking seems to slow down and people start to look at me oddly.

I recall one occasion where I was in a social situation and had been introduced to some friends of a friend of mine. They were all talking to me and my mind just sort of shut down, too much input I guess. I became incoherent and began rambling and I had to leave. This was just so embarrassing. I think that they thought I was on drugs!

With regards to my depression, I think that the reason I became depressed was lack of understanding from other people, including my parents and my brother. My brother in particular looked upon me as an embarrassment and would sometimes deny I was his brother at all.

As a teenager and when I was in my twenties I would spend hours analysing my relationships with others, trying to work out what I was doing wrong. I was constantly rejected, which severely affected my self-esteem.

It was not surprising that I became depressed. Yet when I suggested this as the cause of my depression I was told that this couldn't be the cause. How little did they know?

The anti-depressants helped a bit, along with some counselling, but the counsellor just didn't understand the way I viewed the world. I would patiently explain for instance that when I tried to relate to others it felt like a glass bell jar had been placed over me, cutting me off from other people. I just got blank looks or puzzlement.

I received various diagnoses, such as I was suffering from a number of personality disorders and neuroses. I always knew that they were wrong.

I felt like other people were a different species. As a child I even convinced myself that I was an alien, as it was the only explanation which made sense to me at the time. I was convinced that my parents had adopted me for years, as I was so unlike them.

I am glad that I finally know that I really am different from others. I always knew that I was but no one took me seriously.

I guess over the years I learnt how to deal with my problems to a certain extent. I have come a long way but still have a way to go.

> Iain Payne (UK) Adult with Asperger Syndrome
> (Iain has also been diagnosed as having a number
> of developmental disorders and anxiety)

Change, Change and More Change

Change, change and more change
Of context, place and time.
Why is it that life's transient stage
Plays havoc with my mind?
You said, 'We'll go to McDonald's'
But this was just a thought.
I was set for hours,
But the plan then came to nought.
My tears and confused frustration,
At plans that do not appear,
Are painful beyond recognition
And push me deeper into fear.
How can life be so determined?
How can change be so complete?
With continuity there is no end.
Security and trust are sweet.
So, who said that change would not hurt me?
Who said my 'being' could not be safe?
Change said, 'You need continuity
In order to find your place'.
For change makes all things different,
They no longer are the same.
What was it that you really meant?
All I feel is the pain.

From the book *Life behind Glass*, a personal account
of ASD by Wendy Lawson (Southern Cross University
Press, Lismore, and NSW, Australia)

The Journey

You are driving along a highway,
a caravan of cars – all friends.
Your plan is to stick to the main highway,
your destination is mapped out.
Your car is stopped by an official.
You aren't allowed to continue, you must detour,
turn off onto a dirt track.
'But my friends are on that highway, we're following each
other' you try to explain.
You are disorientated,
and don't want to take the dirt track.
But there's no turning back, the highway is closed to you,
you have no other choice.
The track is bumpy, windy,
and a much longer drive than what was originally planned
for.
You run out of petrol, have flat tyres
and engine failure many times.
You begin to resent your friends who are on the
highway,
why didn't they have to take the detour?
Why are they cruising along?
You eventually get to your destination
and find your friends.
You are now driving side by side in different lanes.
Their trip wasn't as bad as yours, they made it earlier,
but it wasn't without its disruptions either.
You have many stories to share
about your adventurous drive,
and in the end – it has made you a seasoned traveller!

Josie Santomauro

Proud grandparents

We are blessed with 15 grandchildren, which usually earns a double take when we respond with pride to anyone who asks, 'How many grandchildren do you have?' The second question is, 'How many children do you have?' With equal pride, we tick off the names of our five grown children, each of whom is special for different reasons. Our eldest, Mary Ann, is special for many reasons, the most noteworthy of which is that she is the proud mother of an autistic 15-year-old son. For almost as many years, she and her husband, Vince, have been learning, teaching, inspiring and parenting. The produce of their dedication is a handsome young man who can recite Shakespeare and calls me Poppy.

When our grandson was diagnosed with autism we were devastated, frightened and ignorant. He was two when Mary Ann called with the doctor's report. I recall receiving the message from my wife, Marlene. Stunned by what I had just heard, I cancelled the rest of that day's schedule, hurried to my car for the two-hour drive home, and cried most of the way down the New Jersey Turnpike from New York to suburban Philadelphia. How could God do this to us!

We had heard of autism, but we didn't understand the full meaning of the word. My mind was demanding answers, but I had no reliable reference points. Did we know any autistic children or adults? I didn't think so. Would our grandson be physically and mentally disabled, and if so, how severely? I couldn't remember exactly what my wife had told me over the phone. It was as if my mind had exploded for a moment and I had been unable to process the information Marlene was relaying, through the tears of her own anguish as a mother and grandmother.

Coping with the word

As the parents of five, Marlene and I had dealt with our fair share of childhood maladies, ranging from broken bones to dyslexia. We used to joke about being on a first name basis with the medical staff in the emergency room at our local community hospital. The difference was that we were able to get help from experienced professionals who knew how to diagnose and treat the problem, and put our concerns to rest. The words didn't frighten us. Many of the families in our community had children with special needs. But autism? No. Autism was a stranger in our neighborhood.

Our daughter had received her degree in education and had taught at the elementary level in California before returning to the east coast to become a full-time mom of three sons. This last child had seemed unresponsive to normal stimuli before celebrating his second birthday. He was a beautiful child. Other than his apparent lethargy, there was no clue to suggest that there was anything seriously wrong. His hearing had been checked. No problem there. And the pediatrician dismissed the symptoms as a phase. Nothing to worry about.

The worst part has been suspecting something was wrong, and not knowing what that something was. Although we now knew it was autism, it seemed even worse not knowing what the word autism really meant. Not just in medical terms; in terms of quality of life. Marlene said her heart was broken twice: once for our grandson and again for his parents.

Defying the experts

Thanks to our daughter and son-in-law, our grandson was diagnosed early and in the intervening years has received the attention, services, understanding, support and unconditional love he has needed to develop to his full capacity. It hasn't been easy or without strife. Mary Ann's battles with the bureaucracy have been exhausting for her. The 'experts' had advised that their son be institutionalized. Our daughter and son-in-law unequivocally rejected it as an option. The 'experts' had urged that he be placed in special classes for the mentally challenged. His parents insisted that he be tutored and mainstreamed. The 'experts' had predicted that he would be a recluse. They were wrong. In fact, they were wrong on most counts. His mother and father challenged old theories, researched options, demanded answers, confronted the system and met every challenge with confidence in their son, their family and in God.

In May, 1999, our autistic grandson was confirmed in the Catholic faith: a remarkable testament to his parents' love and determination, his two older brothers' understanding and support, his teachers' patience and skill, and his grandparents' prayers and encouragement.

The 'experts' would have been surprised – and, I think, inspired – to see this young man's accomplishments in defiance of what had been the conventional wisdom about autism and its limitations on the human mind and spirit. He participated fully in the liturgy and in the family celebration afterwards. He was in most ways like the other youngsters confirmed that day. But he is, and always will be, autistic.

His most recent accomplishment was last summer. Shakespeare had become one of his favourite authors, so his parents enrolled him in a four-week performing arts program at the local college, which included learning to recite passages from Shakespeare's most popular works. We all crossed our fingers that he would find a way to interact with 50 other performers, five days a week.

And, we thought, it would take a small miracle to persuade him to stand in front of a group and recite anything. How would he deal with the stress?

This was the first summer that our grandson would not have any formal therapy. He had speech and occupational therapy since he was two, year round. Now it was time to see if he could take what had been taught and use it in a setting where no one knew about his difficulties. Could he use the pragmatic skills? Could he read body language of others? Could he carry on a conversation with his peers?

And most of all, could he tolerate the environment with no modifications? Classes were structured, but free time wasn't.

So our daughter set out to make the arrangements to walk her son through the campus several times before the classes began. She made an appointment to meet with the director so her son would know a familiar face beforehand. And, she sat on the campus the first day to assure that all was well.

Our grandson fit in beautifully! He made friends… many of them young ladies who thought he was cute! He expressed the need to be more independent. He went to the university library on his own. He initiated conversations with teachers and peers. And he performed before an audience of strangers.

The big show

The evening of the show featured individual and group performances. We were all crowded into a noisy gym that had been used as a classroom. Surprisingly, our grandson seemed to fit in perfectly with his new friends with whom he had shared the trauma of learning lines and gestures and vocal technique. When it was his turn, front and center, we were astonished. His performance was flawless, worthy of the applause he received, and worthy of the pride that radiated from his parents and grandparents. The best part was that he knew he had accomplished something very difficult, on his own. It was his victory over the limitations of autism.

Mary Ann told us that when he watched himself on video, he became very critical of himself. 'Why does my head bob when I walk?' 'Why do my arms do that?' Now he has a new goal: to imitate proper walking and body posture.

We are constantly amazed at his growing self-awareness and willingness or want to be like his peers. But this is obviously stressful for him, and the extreme effort is noticeable.

It reminds us that he is still autistic, but learning to live with his autism.

Our daughter plans to continue his biofeedback sessions. The training has helped a great deal with stress levels and his social behaviour. Medications were not working and in many cases aggravated his autistic behavior. She sought out a certified EEG Biofeedback specialist and is seeing many changes after just six months of treatment. She believes the training could be one reason her son has been able to do so well this past summer.

Our role as grandparents

We have been fortunate. Our grandson is high functioning. He will go on to college and, with God's grace and his family's continuing support, he will live a productive, independent life. Over the years since that day when we learned of our grandson's special needs, my wife and I have shared the frustration and despair of our daughter's and son-in-law's dark moments, as well as the elation and pride of watching our grandson develop as a functioning person. We have had to learn to be sensitive and caring without being overindulgent. We have become advocates for research into the causes of autism and for parents' and children's rights to educational and medical support services at the local, state and national levels. We have come to respect and revere the parents of autistic children and adults who exhaust themselves for the benefit of others. We have listened to and cheered the parents and grandparents of other autistics in their battle for services desperately needed for optimal physical, mental and emotional development.

We are the proud grandparents of an autistic grandson. And we're looking forward to his next milestone. Something else the experts said he couldn't do.

Tips for grandparents

- Resist the temptation to 'take charge.' Your children (the parents) have the primary and ultimate responsibility to do what they believe is right for the autistic child.

- Own up to reality. We know grandparents who refuse to even talk about their autistic grandson or granddaughter.

- Watch for telltale signs of battle fatigue on the part of your son or daughter (the care providers). Sometimes parenting an autistic becomes overwhelming and they need a break or just a non-judgemental person to talk to.

- Include the autistic grandson or granddaughter like the other grandchildren. Include and involve them in family get togethers.

- As he/she gets older, be prepared to talk with your autistic grandchild about dealing with autism and the effect it may have on life choices. Support the child's parents by being consistent with the counsel they are providing to their autistic son or daughter.

- Take every opportunity to praise your autistic grandchild for each new accomplishment. Show a genuine interest in the grandchild's efforts to develop new skills or improve existing competencies.

- Become an advocate for the rights of all children and adults with special needs. Write letters and give moral support to your children when they do battle with the 'system'.

- Reconcile yourself to the probability that autism will continue to have a profound effect on the lives of your children and your life.

- Investigate the most effective ways to provide financial support from your estate to help support the grandchild's quality of life without making him/her ineligible for federal, state or local services.

- If you believe in a Supreme Being, pray.

By Rick and Marlene Anthony, as appeared in the Nov–Dec 2001 issue of the *Autism Asperger's Digest*, a 52-page bimonthly magazine on autism, see www.autismdigest.com. Reprinted with permission.

Rick and Marlene Anthony are co-founders of iGrandparents.com, and grandparents to 15 grandchildren. They dedicate this column to the thousands of parents, grandparents, children and adults whose lives are affected by autism.

What Now?

What happens once your grandchild is diagnosed?

Generally a chain of events begins where there is a support system set up for your grandchild. Schools may begin to look at the best way to support your grandchild. You may begin to look at the best way of introducing different types of therapy to your grandchild, such as speech therapy and social skills classes. You and the parents may also look at educating yourself in the areas of behaviour management and positive parenting.

Not only will you have the above to contend with, but you will also have the general public, family and friends who may not understand or accept your grandchild's behaviour as a form of disability. They may prefer to judge your grandchild as naughty or spoiled, or proceed to tell you that they 'need a good smack!'

Dealing with family, friends and the public

I used to defend my parenting skills vigilantly! I would be emotionally exhausted. I was trying to justify that my life wasn't as easy as theirs, continually justifying reasons for not attending family functions, etc. Yes, our lives do seem harder, but hey, why do we have to make a song and dance about it? If people are interested, they will ask. So I find now that I only speak about our problems/issues/good news items regarding AS and Damian if I'm asked. I have come to realize that the important thing is that we tell 'ourselves', and listen to 'ourselves'.

'Dear Josie' – an enquiry letter regarding family support

Dear Josie,

Do you have any insights into how to deal with the reactions of extended family and friends? I'm getting mixed responses. Some are supportive and some think it's bunk and that Mike and I just need to parent better. I'm trying to educate and help them, but some things that are being said (and not said) are hurtful. I'm an artist and I'm drawing and painting like mad to alleviate some stress, but would love any advice if you have any.

Thanks, Kate

Hi Kate,

I used to try to do the same thing with educating, etc., but in the end you are running around in circles, ragged, and the people who question your skills seem to be fresh as daisies! The important primary issue is that you, your husband and your child (and any siblings) understand and accept the diagnosis. Who cares about the others – at this stage, anyhow? You have to be very firm and take a stand together as husband and wife, especially when family members make comments regarding your parenting. Don't justify or defend your parenting skills, but keep repeating a phrase that you're comfortable with, e.g. 'He has a mild disability, and we are putting into place strategies to help him for his future.' (Full stop!!) You don't have to explain why, when, how, what or whatever! Be a broken record with your comment, repeat, repeat and repeat. They will eventually get the message that they can't say anything to change you, and one day they may start to show an interest, and that's the key time – when they are interested, it means that they will learn. There's no use trying to teach them now about the disability if they have 'shut-down'.

Don't let any hurtful comments in – put up an invisible shield and see them as scared and frightened people who don't want to accept any changes in 'their' lives. Just know what the truth is, and the truth is that you are doing the best for your child!

Hope this helps. Keep painting!

Josie

The Truth

'You can't tell there's something wrong, are you sure?'
(What makes you suddenly the expert?)
The truth is 'early intervention' and my child's fear of
failure
is what helps him appear 'normal'.

'He has to learn to cope in today's society.'
*(You also can learn to cope with having my child
in your society.)*
The truth is you have to learn compassion.

'That's life! He has to deal with it.'
(Sure, just like you are dealing with his disability.)
The truth is that life *is* hard, show me the ideal person
who can deal with it.

'Don't worry, he'll grow out of it.'
(Not likely!)
The truth is you haven't grown out of your ignorance.

'He manipulates situations.'
(Just like you are trying to do now?)
The truth is you are keen to manipulate my child to
perform.

'You're lucky he's not as bad as some.'
(And you're lucky I forgive you.)
The truth is my child is the lucky one!

Conversation between a mother of a child
with a hidden disability and the world

Josie Santomauro

Awareness

Below is a sample card you can photocopy, cut out, fold in half and glue to carry in your wallet, or you can make up your own cards. This is a great way to create awareness of Asperger Syndrome to strangers and members of the public. Because your grandchild may appear neurotypical members of the public sometimes believe that your grandchild's challenging behaviour is due to behaviour management.

An example of when I used the card was when we were on public transport and Damian was tired, stressed and over-whelmed after a big day out. He wanted to get home and did not have the patience to sit on the bus. He therefore threw a public tantrum and verbally abused me. An elderly couple a few rows down whispered loudly that they thought he needed some discipline. As we approached our stop, I pulled out the card and handed it to them as we hopped off the bus.

Asperger Syndrome affects my grandchild in their communication, behaviour and learning abilities. Therefore my grandchild may experience difficulties in certain social situations. The result being sensory overloads which can sometimes lead to challenging behaviours. We appreciate your patience and understanding.	

Hints, ideas and strategies

- See your grandchild's hobby/obsession as an advantage and use it when trying to put a point across, or when teaching them a strategy or as an incentive in a goal system. E.g. Damian was obsessed with Star Wars, so when we wanted him to be very interested in something we would use Star Wars characters as people or Star Wars computer games as a reward.

- Use language appropriate to your grandchild's understanding – don't go 'over their head' with long descriptive sentences. Keep it short and sweet. E.g. if I asked Damian to do three chores, and instructed them all in a verbal row, he would always hear only the first or the last chore. So now I either write it down for him, or just tell him one at a time.

- Don't all talk at once to the child. This can sound like a muffled room full of people at a party and can be very confusing for the child. It is a good idea for one person to speak at a time, turn taking so the child can listen and absorb the information.

- Use visual charts, timetables, rosters, etc. Damian had a morning and afternoon roster, so he could organize himself to and from school. This helped him become independent and in later years he did not require the visuals any longer as he could think for himself, he had learned it all by rote. When preparing a visual chart, timetable or roster, photographs of the child 'doing' are best, otherwise computer graphics are acceptable.

- When introducing a new activity or routine, draw a 'What do I do' visual story. E.g. in primary school Damian was to catch the school bus on his own. We drew up a visual story with step by step of what he was to do, and this also included some 'what ifs', e.g. what if the bus didn't come, etc. We made a large story about 'Catching the Bus', and also had one reduced down in size for him to keep in his school bag/pocket so he could refer to it. It was a huge success, and he became independent and could catch the bus home like other, neurotypical children.

- Set realistic, achievable goals for your grandchild. When setting goals check whether they are achievable by your grandchild, as every child's progress is different. Also does the main goal need to be broken down into smaller goals first before it can be achieved?

- Do not join the 'angry game'. When a situation is escalating, send your grandchild to time out and walk away, have a cup of tea and wait at least half an hour for emotions to settle down before dealing with the problem. I find that if Damian comes home with a dark mood, I leave him alone for at least half an hour. He goes straight to his room, then when he has had downtime he emerges to talk to me. If I am in his face when I know that he is in a dark mood, then he will just become aggravated and take his day's frustrations out on me.

- If you feel that all is failing, please don't hesitate to ask for help, don't wait for issues to escalate and possibly get out of control. There are various avenues of help: Parent-line, support groups, school counsellor, etc. Do not think that asking for help is a sign of failure. It is a sign of strength to ask for help as you are looking at solutions and not burying your head in the sand.

- Play games with your grandchild to encourage turn taking, etc. Some great games are simple board games and some card games.

- Listen to yourself – are you using positive talk? Sometimes we need to hear ourselves and others around us – are we speaking positively or negatively? If we expect these children to learn to be positive, then we need to model this behaviour.

- Eventually, the parents will need to share the diagnosis with your grandchild. They will know when they are both ready. Be supportive and patient. It is very important to wait until the child is ready. There is no use in giving information when it is not required, as this can sometimes overwhelm a child who previously thought there was nothing wrong or different. There will come a day, whether the child is eight or eighteen, when they will begin to question their difference.

- If you notice your grandchild becoming distressed, you can remind them to take themselves to time out or a quiet area to wind down. Sometimes it is best to give them a wide berth to calm down – do not attempt to deal with a situation as it is happening unless there is an issue with safety. It's always a good idea to give them time to wind down.

- Remind your grandchild to look at their charts and timetables. If you are aware that they are struggling with a challenge and they do have a chart/timetable with that scenario, a gentle prompt is beneficial to remind them they have visual cues to help.

- Remind them of any changes or new things that are going to happen, like birthdays or lessons. Sometimes we get so caught up in what is going to happen or preparing to go somewhere that we forget to inform the child that they are included. If they have a whiteboard calendar, talk to them about it and add it to the calendar. And a reminder the day before as well as on the day is helpful also.

- Warn your grandchild about changes they don't know about. Changes are hard for children with AS, in particular if they were looking forward to going somewhere. It can be a huge let down as they have planned the scenario over and over in their heads. So if they were looking forward to seeing the real pirate at the pirate party and then you arrive and the pirate is not coming because he is sick, take the child to a quiet area and explain calmly what has happened. Sometimes we do not know how they will react. They may accept this information or they may be triggered into a tantrum. Use behavioural management strategies if the latter happens.

- Try to tell them all about where you are going or what is about to happen. Even draw a picture for them, or write down what you know. E.g. when Damian was to attend his first school camp we went for a drive and took him to the grounds, walked around, showed him the rooms, where they would eat, etc. He also took photos and showed his class that week. We glued the photos to a chart, so he could become familiar with the campgrounds. The result was a successful camp!

- Asperger Syndrome does not mean all doom and gloom – you can have a healthy relationship with your grandchild. Children with Asperger Syndrome have a wonderful sense of humour. Laugh and have fun with them.

Sacred Support

Support is indeed sacred. Although the journey will be made mostly with immediate family, it's important to have others who you can rely on, talk with or to be there to listen to you. Trying to do this with friends or family who don't fully understand your situation is sometimes hard. This is when support groups can be called upon.

Meeting other parents and grandparents with ASD children is like meeting people who have a similar cultural background to you. They understand our language, our needs, our emotional rollercoaster rides, our difficulties within society and most importantly, they understand our children.

Support groups

Individual support groups may operate differently to each other, but these are the basic aims of an Asperger Syndrome support group:

- to provide support to families and the individual with AS

- to provide information on Asperger Syndrome to parents and professionals

- to provide a resource library which includes books, videos, etc.

- to educate the community on Asperger Syndrome

- to organize workshops, seminars and guest speakers.

You can also visit the following very informative and helpful websites:

MAAP Services for Autism and Asperger Syndrome – a non-profit organization providing information to families of individuals with autism, AS and pervasive developmental disorder. www.asperger.org

National Autistic Society, UK – provides help, support and services to individuals with autism and their families. www.nas.org.uk

Dr Tony Attwood – the world-renowned clinical psychologist's guide for parents, professionals and people with AS and their partners.
www.tonyattwood.com.au

Asperger Services Australia – claiming to be the world's largest support group for AS, they provide support to parents, families, carers and siblings as well as to children, adolescents and adults with AS.
www.asperger.asn.au

Josie Santomauro – author and presenter on AS, Josie also writes children's fiction under the name Josie Montano.
www.booksbyjosie.com.au

OASIS – Online Asperger Syndrome Information and Support.
www.aspergersyndrome.org

The End?

Of course it's not the end.

Unfortunately we sometimes tend to only hear the difficult and heart wrenching stories about having a grandchild with Asperger Syndrome. Laura Gilbert shares with us her son's success story; she says, 'I believe that parents and children are mutual gifts to each other.' I believe she's right! It's all about how we perceive situations brought into our lives.

I have come to understand that it's whether you perceive the gift as a problem...or the problem as a gift...

Mutual gifts

At 15, our son is now a very articulate, witty and socially aware adolescent. After all the counselling that he has had, covering the range from psychological self-help strategies to social skill development, in many ways he is now actually more sophisticated in understanding himself and others than many of his peers.

He now has a circle of friends that he developed on his own, makes honour roll every marking period, and requires no medication nor special help in school. He has never loved school, but functions well within the school environment and often with a sense of humour.

Since art is his forte and his passion, we tell him to be patient until the day that he can devote most of his time doing what he loves.

As with all of us, our son is still a 'work in progress'. But I've come to realize that through his fears, phobias and social misperceptions, I have learned and grown and become more than I ever was before. I believe that parents and children are mutual gifts to each other. We are given, in this life, exactly what we need to become all that we are truly meant to be.

Laura Gilbert (USA) Mother
of a teenager with Asperger Syndrome